S H E E R

Martha Collins

BARNWOOD PRESS
2008

My thanks to the following publications, in which these poems first appeared: *AGNI, American Poetry Review, Boulevard, Denver Quarterly, Great River Review, Iowa Review, The Journal, Orion, Paris Review, Pleiades, The Progressive, Solo, TriQuarterly, Virginia Quarterly Review, Witness.* Some of the poems also appeared in *The Extraordinary Tide: New Poetry by American Women,* ed. Susan Aizenberg and Erin Belieu (Columbia).

"As Boats, Over That Darkness" is for May Stevens, "Out of My Own Pocket" is in memory of Paula Rankin, and "Their Houses There Without Their Bodies" is in memory of Alan Glovsky. My gratitude to these artists and friends, and to Eva Hesse and Ann Healy, whose works in the Oberlin College Allen Memorial Art Museum inspired other poems in this collection.

"As If You Had Promised" is for Ted Space.

Cover Art: Michael Mazur, *Winter I* (1990)
     12 x 12 inches, monotype on silk, collection of the artist
Author Photo: Betsy Molnar
Book Design: Steve Farkas

First Printing

ISBN-13: 978-0-935306-54-5
ISBN-10: 0-935306-54-4

The Barnwood Press
4604 47th Avenue S
Seattle WA 98117
www.barnwoodpress.org

for Pamela Alexander

Contents

SHEER

Out of My Own Pocket

Light drifts from the stalled
Aegean ships to the bare table

where pages rise in a brief
breeze, then fall, opened palms

after a prayer. What
is required this time? Paid

my dues. Pain was referred
to another place. Point by point.

Settled in by the leaded
window. Wind out of my sails.

Then I considered the shape
I was in. Out of my own

pocket, I said, offering pure
air, all done with tiny mirrors

sewn into the cloth.
Nothing now but to turn

the page, and then I hear *In my
book,* the voice not mine but

mine the slipping down
again, slope, shaft, strip, old

bones preserved, pressed
into the coal. Not the girl,

not even the wailing mother,
harbored rage trailing

the shimmering ships, and not
the ships or the whispering

sea, but a woman turning away
from the crowd, taking her keys

from her pocket, a woman
on her way, on her way home.

That Time

The trees were filled with tiny worms — caterpillars, I guess — that hung
    down on invisible threads.

How'd it go? she asked her friend, who was drawing a blue line on her lid.

The ground colors were something else: goldenrod, asters, Queen Anne's
    lace, fields of yellowing beans.

Seeds, of course, maple wings, and yellow dust in the air.

He handed me a red rose, open except for two petals that covered its
    sex like hands.

Yellow butterflies, white butterflies, baby snake on the path.

Do you want to? he asked, and I wasn't sure.

When the child came in from play, it was almost dark.

Transgression

thick green thighs birch bones shining
through is she trying to hide them

you have been (blank)ing too much
he said, no he said the word

her did he know it
was her her just-mussed hair

her first her

———

raccoon raccoon deer something
red ripped at eaten meat

salt pepper landscape
in the notebook *willow bird*

how do you say does one say is it said

then the knife

face mouth eye

———

a line crossed a wall
walked through: no road

as if no one ever had done

been died no bones in the soil

knife perhaps in the picnic
basket pictures apparatus

someone related

———

slipped comma hook without
its arm scythe suspended

over hills that hide

nest of time where no one
misses guesses yet

anyone ever

later a loss of mind

Inside the Body the Snakes

but which are the snakes and which

is the body and who is doing

inside the body the turning the snakes

have gone inside what is or might

be the body the snakes are eating

from inside the body out and daring

with information perhaps to turn

or begin to turn the body but what

is the information they're looking

over from inside the upright that is

the body whatever it is the snakes

are turning outside and stretching

the frame and slipping the body down

toward the ground that is also body

From One

One becoming less
than one. Some were never
so much. Remember this
is not—

Two born together shared
a heart. One to give, one
to take. Oh *no*. But why
not? Had names.

Face goes. Nose
nothing. Mouth teeth. Eye
something else, eye absence
of eye, surrounded.

No one becomes
nothing. Rather many: much
work to do to pull itself
apart, eye to pull

back from ~~yellow *ginestra* lining~~
the ~~folds of~~ hills, ~~silver~~
~~filigree of olive trees,~~ late
afternoon, way

back, late
for later, ~~lizard skimming~~
~~the pebbled path,~~ cross
it strike it, no

wonder, what is so
what is nothing new but comes
a time when heart itself
would be taken.

Like Her Body the World

hit and hit and hit and hit and fallen

getting up and trying to get up

now one part is hitting another part wounding its flesh

slicing its own veins breaking its bones

but wait we are coming help is on the way

now we are hitting the part that is hitting the part

now someone else is helping the part we hit

now it is arm against arm hand against hand

now it is eye against eye no one can see

now it is ear against ear there is no mouth

where is the up to get up to where is the body

where are the parts have the parts all fallen apart

we are part of the body we forgot

we thought we lived outside like a brain in a jar

we thought we were pure like thought with nothing to lose

but we are losing too we are losing parts

besides we were never that brain we were only a part

we thought we would never fall but we are falling

falling and falling and falling hitting the air

falling hitting ourself our own body

meanwhile the body the world will try to get up

or else the body the world will lie down will lie down

Of Blood

drop   stream   fountain
in the hymn filled with Jesus

a woman who'd known blood
as a sweet release

in the park filled with martyrs'
spilled for God red fountain

woke with hands he had a gun
woke with hands around my neck

———

a war was on as one might say
a television was on and it

to shed one's own clothing skin
to shed someone else's blood

gray faces gray bodies
always on, that naked child

bodies running falling stopped
black blood on the screen

———

on a boat on a moonlit river a man
whose poems were slipped from prison

while another man made war
from a boat in that distant country

word by word the first man sings
now while the other man tries to fish

in his country our country he
sees blood running over the deck

———

in that other country women fought
they wrote they knew blood as loss

I didn't know I wanted I took
a notebook he had a gun

felt like a war why should there be
war blood on our hands mine

imagined my hands dripping
with blood gripping his neck

The Bombs

We hit the train we are sorry it was a mistake.

We hit those refugees sorry another mistake.

We hit the bridge there were people we couldn't see.

We hit the water supply not a mistake but we are sorry.

We hit the embassy sorry another mistake.

We hit the wrong country it wasn't planned.

In the past we have also hit the wrong things a passenger plane a school.

This time the reasons for hitting what we were trying to hit were good.

We were trying to stop the terrible things being done to innocent people.

Things got worse for those people after we started which proves we
    were right.

But of course we cannot think about what is right or what is wrong.

They call us smart but bombs are not made to think.

We are sorry there were mistakes but we ourselves make no mistakes.

We only follow orders. We do what we're told.

Glyphs

1

a woman strokes her finger with her finger

let's have a look inside, he said

a man strokes the sides of his new moustache

but I have worn the wrong clothes

wasn't the doctor, was it, one

snow down there, under the clouds

middle finger, index finger

sewed the wrong season, seam

heart, anchor around her neck

who came with his fat black bag

2

a woman makes tiny cuts on her arm

please do not think we do not care

a man tears at his nails with his nails

this is the way the bomb works

do you bury it, use it, or store it and wait?

the most devoted years of your life

please do not climb on Little Boy

a half-life of 24,000

shards arranged on a flat rock

what do you do with your rage?

3

bitten thumb

to be in touch with

sucked in held in air

nonetheless there are animals in the

what if there's no (something) there

under your desks, the turtle said

and then the forest filled with knives

sky flashed with fire when I was

what if there's no way to (something)

keep watching this spot

4

what is touched?

things we have done, left, undone

who are we inviting in?

once I imagined an animal skull

unforgettable hair, the color of apricots

sweater like the one I lost

goat calf lamb where my heart

a new element

please note here

inscriptions in a cave

5

hands at rest

do not disturb do not deface

not a smile exactly, but

just before the top of a hill

all right, going to be

artifacts pottery animals plants

the sky deepens, a deeper blue

have found a use for

someone else

because of the red road

6

hand on hand on hand on

here today gone to

mouth to mouth to mouth

mountain bluebird flew across

puckered a little, where river seams

waves riding under us over us wind

fields of spring snow

new bed, where no one else

snug little house at the end

coming soon

All for Now

Because when we fell from our beds
there was no one to catch us, when we knelt

in our troubled fields we had no thought
of descending wings, extended arms.

Because in that white sky there was no
discernible source of light, because the only

proof of light was our own scarcely
visible shadows, we turned to them, took

their vague hands in ours, let our bodies
fall into their bodies. And let it be said:

we were comforted as we held ourselves,
comforted that it was ourselves we held.

Sometimes it seemed, not as if we were not
enough, but as if something wanted

us, waited for us. And once we tried, in the dim
light, to read the strange lines carved on stones

found by the river. But the words, if there had
been words, belonged to the water.

Then, early one dawn when the thick sky
hovered close to our heads, ponds of mist

rose from the ponds beside our road,
and down through clouds came faint

lights, outlining birds, like constellations.
Planes, someone said, and that was all.

But they stayed with us, those shapes
of rising mist, those bodiless birds.

Sheer, If We Could Be

The premise is silk.

The argument gathers, long and narrow.

Tall and slim, but not slight.

Terrain, hills, rivers. Chinese ink.

As if we were drawn.

In shadow, it takes shape, admits space.

Like a photograph, but not of itself.

Lighter and darker, with pockets, places to rest.

As our shadows would be, if we could be seen through.

Dress wearing itself, covering nothing.

Draped suggestion.

Not concluded: position could shift.

Not to be done.

Ourselves suspended.

Bad Air

1

no one is climbing the mountain

streaks of red on the heaving chest

no snow blowing over tracks in the snow

severed flesh on a serving dish

general, over the whole and the part

an O without a

weapons in the sky

2

someone's messing around up there

the beautiful view from the beautiful roof

who slept with who slept with who slept with

gotta be, or things'd be

of buildings filled with money and its

gods stand up

what if someone pushed

3

can't see it taste it smell it but

wouldn't believe the things they said

keeps pushing things around, but

didn't happen, and if it did

mussing the water's thin dress

cannot be such a monster

nothing in writing

4

face to face to face to

as if the sky had opened above our

just a friendly conversation

filled with flying creatures, clouds

knives and forks in the proper hands but

good I mean to do

simply said

5

everyone breathed a little sigh

blue came in, between the trees

after that night on the mountain we

like spaces filled in a coloring book

anger to wisdom, poison to medicine

sleep till we wake them

snakes curled up in jars

As Boats, Over That Darkness

The underboat is upside down, blurred, like a reflection.

The reflection of a bridge that isn't there.

The underboat is flanked by shapes like the underbanks of a wide canal.

The shapes point, like the bows of boats.

They point to small boats that glide on the water.

The underboat is under the boats.

The boats are surrounded by waves of words.

The words are golden light, on the dark of the water.

The boats move in and out of the words, revealing other colors, blues, greens.

The boats are separate, small, but they find a path, like a flock of birds.

Their oars are wings, folded, lifted, falling.

The boats are gliding through, into the light.

The golden sea pressing down on the undersea.

The undersea holding it up.

From the Sky

> Snow is expected to fall from the sky.
> —*Boston Globe*, March 1999

Snow will fall from the sky
Snow will turn to rain
Rain will fill our streams
The earth will turn again

Snow will turn to rain
Blossoms will fill the trees
The earth will turn again
Petals will fill the air

Blossoms will fill the trees
Petals will fall like snow
Petals will fill the air
Green will fill the trees

Petals will fall like snow
Petals will fall to earth
Green will fill the trees
Where air was, leaves will be

Petals will fall to earth
Leaves will fall from trees
Where air was, leaves will be
Leaves, where there was snow

Leaves will fall from trees
Colors will brighten the air
Leaves, where there was snow
Leaves will fall to earth

Colors will brighten the air
Like hair and blood and skin
Leaves will fall to earth
Where we will fall from our lives

Like hair and blood and skin
Leaves will turn to earth
Where we will fall from our lives
Where we were, air will be

Leaves will turn to earth
Rain will fill our streams
Where we were, air will be
Snow will fall from the sky

Their Houses There Without Their Bodies

no one is there but someone will be there

transparent houses that have no rooms

or someone was there and is coming back

that have no walls there is nothing but air

or someone is there but can't be seen

or is it water that bubbling that blue

they are not there but they seem to be diving

their clothes are clinging to transparent walls

or swimming in underwater houses

their silvery coppery chairs are balanced

their houses are breathing water their arms

their chairs their jackets their hats are waiting

their bodies cannot be seen they are sitting

and breathing without their bodies they are home

As If You Had Promised

not to steer but to steady
the boat when I steer into un-

when I steer into strange

when strange comes, bidden or un-

to be the water that rocks
the boat to dreams
that tell the poor

truth another
truth, let it slip

as water slips
into water

to be the shore that gives

the shore that takes

the shore that holds
the hands
of waves lets

the waves take
its body gives
them body

to be the house the house
I am stands next
to, space between

us filled
with space

not to build but to be
the house come home to

Benediction

Not a story, they said, not even a line.

And there wasn't a line, there was a circle.

A perfect circle, though there were breaks.

But it wasn't broken, it was open.

It was open in the spaces between—

It was open in the spaces between them.

And they were like candles, giving light.

But the light came from the length of their bodies.

And they were like lilies, that opened their throats.

And as they opened they almost touched.

And they threw back their heads, and the circle widened.

And there was silence, but they were singing.